Tools for Problem Solving

Level D

STECK-VAUGHN
COMPANY

A Division of Harcourt Brace & Company

Acknowledgments

Executive Editor	Diane Sharpe
Senior Project Editor	Donna Rodgers
Editor	Allison Welch
Design Project Manager	Sheryl Cota
Cover Design	John Harrison
Electronic Production	PC&F, Inc.
Photography	Cover: © David B. Fleetham/Animals Animals; p.1 © David B. Fleetham/Animals Animals; p.18 © Stephen Whalen/The Viesti Collection; p.19 © Roy Morsch/The Stock Market; p.20 (t) © Kathy Ferguson/PhotoEdit; p.24 (b) © Michael Newman/ PhotoEdit; p.34 © Joe Viesti/The Viesti Collection; p.44 © Bill Truslow/Tony Stone; p.46 (b) © Robert Ginn/PhotoEdit; p.47 © Michael Lewis/Corbis; p.52 © Tony Freeman/PhotoEdit; p.66 (t, m) © PhotoDisc; p.67 © Robert Pearcy/Animals Animals; p.70 (t) © PhotoDisc; p.76 (t) © Tony Freeman/PhotoEdit; p.77 (b) © Kathleen Campbell/Tony Stone; p.80 (r) © Reed/Williams/ Animals Animals; Additional photography by Digital Studios.
Illustration	pp. 4–17 Bill Ogden; pp. 22, 27, 28, 30, 33, 42, 43, 44, 57 Dave Blanchette.

Contents

Lesson 1 Write a Plan

Suppose you and your family were traveling by wagon on the Oregon Trail. You plan to go from The Dalles to Fort Bridger. What is the total distance you will travel?

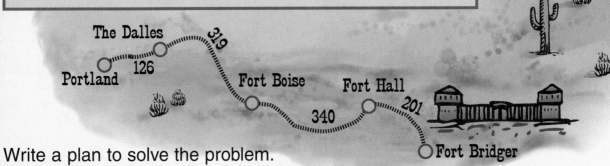

Write a plan to solve the problem.

Step 1 Write in your own words what you need to find out.

_____

_____

Step 2 Write the facts that will be useful.

_____

_____

Step 3 Explain or show how you will solve the problem.

_____

_____

_____

_____

_____

_____

_____

Make a Model

Try using base ten blocks to solve the problem.

> **U**se the blocks to show the distance between each town. Add and regroup the blocks if you need to. What is the total distance in miles from The Dalles to Fort Bridger?

Remember:
10 ones = 1 tens strip
10 tens = 1 hundreds flat

1. Model the distance from The Dalles to Fort Boise using hundreds flats, tens strips, and ones cubes.

    _____ hundreds _____ tens _____ ones

2. Model the distance from Fort Boise to Fort Hall.

    _____ hundreds _____ tens _____ ones

3. Model the distance from Fort Hall to Fort Bridger.

    _____ hundreds _____ tens _____ ones

4. Add the ones. How many ones are there in all? _____ ones

    Regroup. _____ tens _____ ones

5. Add the tens. How many are there in all? _____ tens

6. Add the hundreds. How many are there in all? _____ hundreds

7. What is the total distance from The Dalles to Fort Bridger? _____ miles

Practice

Here are three problems for you.

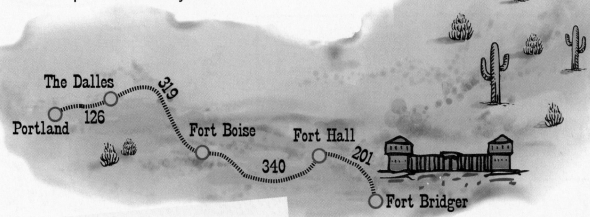

The Dalles
319
Portland 126
Fort Boise
Fort Hall
340
201
Fort Bridger

Quick-Solve 1

Look at the map. Is it farther from Portland to Fort Boise, or from Fort Boise to Fort Bridger?

Quick-Solve 2

One family traveled 117 miles the first week of their trip. They went 106 miles the next week. How many miles did they travel in two weeks?

Quick-Solve 3

In 1845, what supplies might you buy if you had $169.00?

Farming Supplies, 1845	
Span of horses	$100.00
Cow	$15.00
Double wagon	$50.00
Shovel	$2.00
Log chains	$4.00
Hammer and nails	$1.00

Use What You Know

If you live in Chimney Rock, how far away is your grandmother in Independence, Missouri?

> Use the blocks to show the distance between each town. Add and regroup the blocks if you need to. What is the total distance in miles from Chimney Rock to Independence?

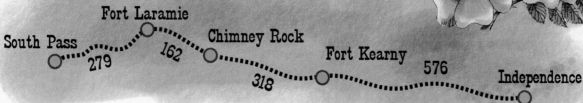

South Pass
Fort Laramie
279
162
Chimney Rock
318
Fort Kearny
576
Independence

1. Model the distance from Chimney Rock to Fort Kearny using hundreds flats, tens strips, and ones cubes.

   _____ hundreds   _____ tens   _____ ones

2. Model the distance from Fort Kearny to Independence.

   _____ hundreds   _____ tens   _____ ones

3. Add the ones. How many ones are there in all?   _____ ones

   Regroup.   _____ tens   _____ ones

4. Add the tens. How many are there in all?   _____ tens

5. Add the hundreds. How many are there in all?   _____ hundreds

6. How far away is Chimney Rock from Independence?   _____ miles

7. Mr. Kendall said sadly, "My grandchildren moved 1,000 miles away from my home in Independence." Between which two towns along the trail do his grandchildren live? How do you know?

_____

_____

Lesson 2 Write a Plan

Two Pony Express riders plan to meet in Fort Bridger. One of the riders will come from Smith Creek and the other from Fort Laramie. How much farther will the rider from Smith Creek ride than the one from Fort Laramie?

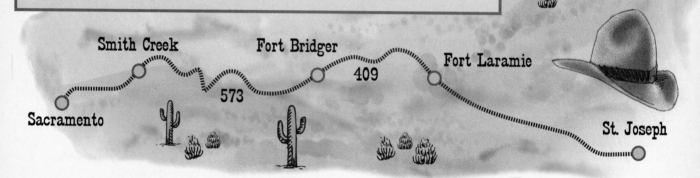

Write a plan to solve the problem.

Step 1

Write in your own words what you need to find out.

_____

_____

Step 2

Write the facts that will be useful.

_____

_____

Step 3

Explain or show how you will solve the problem.

_____

_____

_____

_____

_____

_____

_____

Writing a Plan: Subtracting 3- and 4-Digit Numbers

Make a Model

Try using base ten blocks to solve the problem.

Remember:
6 tens 13 ones is the same as 7 tens 3 ones.

Use the blocks to show the distance between each town. Regroup the blocks if you need to. How much longer is the distance from Smith Creek to Fort Bridger than the distance from Fort Laramie to Fort Bridger?

1. Model the number of miles in the greater distance using hundreds flats, tens strips, and ones cubes.

   _____ hundreds _____ tens _____ ones

2. Subtract blocks equal to the number of miles in the shorter distance. Regroup if you need to.

3. How many hundreds, tens, and ones are left?

   _____ hundreds _____ tens _____ ones

4. How much longer is the distance of Fort Bridger to Smith Creek than Fort Bridger to Fort Laramie?   _____ miles

5. The distance from Sacramento to Fort Bridger is 885 miles. Look at the map on page 8. Find the distance from Sacramento to Smith Creek.   _____ miles

6. The first Pony Express trip was in April, 1860. How many years ago was the first trip?   _____ years

Practice

Here are three problems for you.

Quick-Solve 1

One Pony Express rider traveled 601 miles in a week. Another rider traveled 453 miles. How much farther did the first rider travel?

Quick-Solve 2

One rider earned $325 in three months. Another rider earned $295 in three months. How much more did the first rider earn?

WANTED

Skinny wiry fellows not over eighteen.
Must be expert riders willing
to risk death daily.
Orphans preferred.
WAGES $25 each week.

Quick-Solve 3

After riding 78 miles as fast as he could, the Pony Express rider rested at a station. He rode 6 different horses. He rode the first horse 15 miles, the second 15 miles, the third 14 miles, and the fourth 10 miles. He rode the fifth and sixth horses each the same distance. How far did he ride the sixth horse?

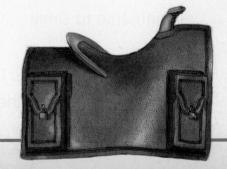

Use What You Know

Suppose a Pony Express rider stopped 84 miles west of Smith Creek to get out of a storm. How many more miles is it to Sacramento?

> **U**se the blocks to show the total distance and the distance from Smith Creek to Sacramento. Subtract the number of miles traveled so far. Regroup the blocks if you need to. How many miles are left?

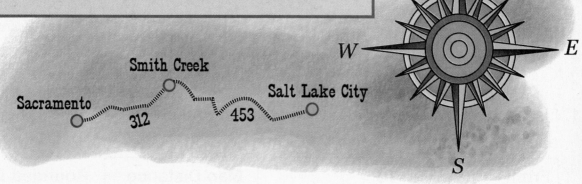

1. Model the number of miles from Smith Creek to Sacramento using hundreds flats, tens strips, and ones cubes.

   _____ hundreds   _____ tens   _____ ones

2. Subtract blocks equal to the number of miles the rider went before stopping for shelter. Regroup if you need to.

3. How many hundreds, tens, and ones are left?

   _____ hundreds   _____ tens   _____ ones

4. How many more miles will the rider travel to arrive in Sacramento?   _____ miles

5. A rider going from Salt Lake City to Sacramento camped 218 miles west of Salt Lake City. Put a mark on the map to show about where he set up camp. How many more miles will he need to ride to complete his trip?   _____ miles

Lesson 3 Make an Estimate

You have made a model to solve problems.
Now try making an estimate to solve a problem.

> **W**as the total distance of the Pony Express greater than or less than 1,700 miles? How do you know?

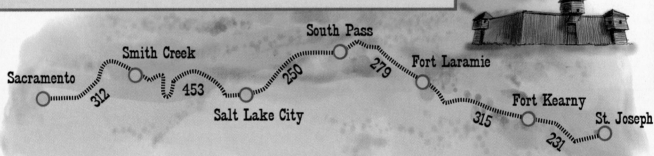

1. List all the distances between the stations. Round each number to the nearest 100. Then add.

From	To	Map Distance	Rounded Distance
St. Joseph	Ft. Kearny	231	200
Ft. Kearny	Ft. Laramie		
Ft. Laramie	South Pass		
South Pass	Salt Lake City		
Salt Lake City	Smith Creek		
Smith Creek	Sacramento		

= about _____

2. The Pony Express was _____ (greater, less) than 1,700 miles.

3. Between which two stations was about halfway on the Pony Express? How do you know?

_____

_____

Making an Estimate: Adding 3-Digit Numbers

Practice

Here are three practice problems for you.

Sacramento — 312 — Smith Creek — 453 — Salt Lake City — 250 — South Pass — 279 — Fort Laramie — 315 — Fort Kearny — 231 — St. Joseph

Quick-Solve 1

Use the map to find two stations that are about 1,000 miles apart.

Quick-Solve 2

Use the map. Suppose each Pony Express rider could ride about 100 miles a day. If each rider rode only once, would 16 riders be enough for the entire journey?

Quick-Solve 3

A family traveling from Minnesota to Montana bought food for the trip. Into their wagon, they packed this food. How many pounds of food did they load on the wagon?

> 675 lb flour
>
> 450 lb sugar
>
> 280 lb of cornmeal
>
> 50 lb each of beans, cheese, butter

Use What You Know

You learned how to make an estimate with addition.
Now try making an estimate with subtraction.

> If you were on the Oregon Trail at The Dalles, about
> how much farther would you have to go to Portland?

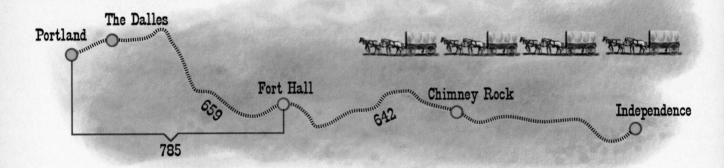

1. List the distances between the stations. Round each number to
   the nearest 100. Then subtract.

From	To	Map Distance	Rounded Distance
Fort Hall	Portland		
Fort Hall	The Dalles		

= about _____

2. About how far was The Dalles to Portland? _____ miles

3. If you traveled about 19 miles a day, could you go from
   The Dalles to Portland in a week? How do you know?

   _____

   _____

4. The Oregon Trail was about 2,000 miles long. About how far
   was Chimney Rock from Independence? How do you know?

   _____

   _____

Lesson 4   Solve It Your Way

Read each problem and decide how you will find the solution.

Use the map to solve the problems.

**Make a Model
Make an Estimate**

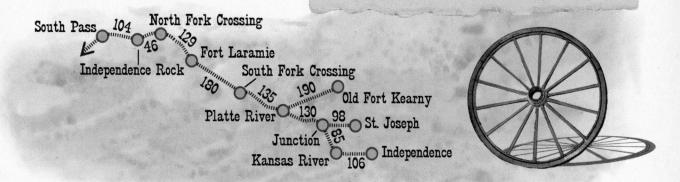

1. How much farther is Independence to Junction than St. Joseph to Junction?

2. How far is Fort Laramie to South Pass?

3. At South Fork Crossing, the wagon leader says you have traveled exactly 450 miles from Independence. Is he right? How do you know?

4. A wagon train plans to rest for a week about 300 miles away from Old Fort Kearny. At which station will they rest?

5. Suppose riders changed horses about every 12 miles. About how many horses would be needed between Platte River and South Fork Crossing?

6. The Pony Express has 9 riders waiting to carry the mail from St. Joseph to South Pass. If each rider can travel about 100 miles, will there be enough riders? How do you know?

Practice

Now write your own problems using addition and subtraction:

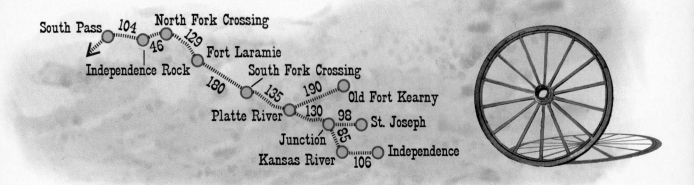

Quick-Solve 1
The answer to the problem is "Fort Laramie is about halfway." Write your own problem to share with a friend.

Quick-Solve 2
The answer to the problem is "The distance is less than 100 miles shorter." Write your own problem to share with a friend.

Quick-Solve 3
The answer to the problem is "The distance is about 100 miles longer." Write your own problem to share with a friend.

Review   Show What You Know

Work in a small group. Use the map of the California Trail through the Rocky Mountains.

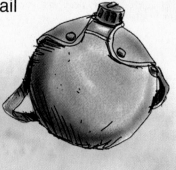

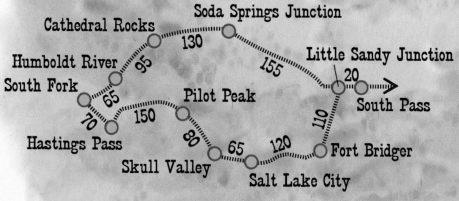

Soda Springs Junction

Cathedral Rocks
130

Humboldt River   95   Little Sandy Junction
South Fork   65   155   20
70   Pilot Peak   South Pass
150   110
Hastings Pass   80   65   120   Fort Bridger
Skull Valley   Salt Lake City

Find the routes from South Pass to Hastings Pass.

1. What is the distance of the north trail? _____ miles

2. What is the distance of the south trail? _____ miles

3. Write your own addition and subtraction problems using distances on the map. Share your problems with another group. Ask them to solve them.

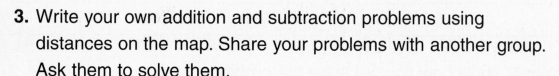

_____

_____

_____

_____

_____

_____

UNIT 2 What's My Number?

Lesson 1 Write a Plan

Marcus and Janet are playing *What's My Number?* Marcus begins with 3, 14, 25. He asks Janet, "What's my next number?" How will Janet answer?

Write a plan to solve the problem.

Step 1 Write in your own words what you need to find out.

_____

_____

Step 2 Write the facts that will be useful.

_____

_____

Step 3 Explain or show how you will solve the problem.

_____

_____

_____

_____

_____

_____

Writing a Plan: Mixed Operations

Find a Pattern

You can find a pattern to solve the problem.

> **W**rite the numbers Marcus gave. Look for a number pattern. Use the pattern to guess Janet's answer.

1. Write Marcus's numbers.

   _____ , _____ , _____

2. Will the next number in the game be greater than or less than 25? How do you know?

   _____

   _____

   _____

3. What is the difference between 3 and 14? _____

4. What is the difference between 14 and 25? _____

5. What is the pattern? How do you know?

   _____

   _____

   _____

6. How will Janet answer? _____

Practice

Here are three practice problems for you.

Quick-Solve 1

In the next *What's My Number?* game, Janet says, "22, 29, 36, and 43." Find the pattern. What number will Janet say next?

Quick-Solve 2

Ashley plays *What's My Number?* She says, "2, 6." Then she says, "The next number is not 12 or 18." What is the next number?

Quick-Solve 3

When Ashley said, "The next number is not 12 or 18," what was she thinking? What is the pattern in 2, 6, 12? What about 2, 6, 18? What might come next in each?

Applying Strategies

Use What You Know

Here is another *What's My Number?* game to play.

> **J**essica begins with 40, 31, 22. She asks Grady, "What is my next number?" How will Grady answer?

If you need help, look back to page 19.

1. Write Jessica's numbers.

_____ , _____ , _____

2. Will the next number in the game be greater than or less than 22? How do you know?

_____

_____

3. What is the difference between 40 and 31? _____

4. What is the difference between 31 and 22? _____

5. What is the pattern? How do you know?

_____

_____

6. How will Grady answer? _____

Lesson 2 Write a Plan

Now Fran and Carlos are playing the *What's My Number?* game. Look at their conversation. If Fran says 6 next, what will Carlos say?

Write a plan to solve the problem.

Step 1 Write in your own words what you need to find out.

_____

_____

Step 2 Write the facts that will be useful.

_____

_____

Step 3 Explain or show how you will solve the problem.

_____

_____

_____

_____

_____

_____

Writing a Plan: Mixed Operations

Find a Pattern

Look for number patterns.

This time look for patterns within a pattern.

> Look again at the conversation. Look for more than one pattern. Use it to predict Carlos's next answer.

1. What is Fran's pattern?

   _____

2. What is Carlos's pattern?

   _____

3. What is the relationship between 9 and 27? 8 and 24?
   7 and 21? Is it the same for each pair?

   _____

   _____

4. What will Carlos's answer be when Fran says 6? How
   do you know?

   _____

   _____

5. Write three more pairs of numbers Fran and Carlos
   might say.

   _____   _____

   _____   _____

   _____   _____

Practice

Here are three practice problems for you.

Quick-Solve 1

Jeff's telephone number is 161–3107. He writes his number as 16, 13, 10, 7. He notices a pattern. What rule can Jeff use to remember his telephone number?

Quick-Solve 2

Imagine you can hear only part of a *What's My Number?* game. When Daniel says 3, Samantha answers 18. Would you be able to find the pattern? Explain why or why not.

Quick-Solve 3

Heather wrote a pattern with a missing number. Find the missing number and name the pattern.

512, 128,————, 8, 2

Applying Strategies

Use What You Know

Look for number patterns.

If you need help, look back to page 23.

> Fran and Carlos play another game. The numbers are 48 and 8, 36 and 6, 24 and 4. What is the next pair of numbers?

1. What is the pattern of the first number in each pair?

_____

2. What is the pattern of the second number in each pair?

_____

3. What is the relationship between 48 and 8? 36 and 6? 24 and 4? Is it the same for each pair?

_____

_____

4. What is the next pair of numbers? How do you know?

_____

_____

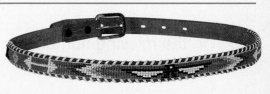

5. Carlos says that the final pair would be 0 and 0. Do you agree? Explain why or why not.

_____

_____

_____

Lesson 3   Use Logical Reasoning

You have found a pattern to solve problems.
Now try using logical reasoning to play
What's My Number?

You may want to make your own number cards.

Fran and Grady make up a new game.
They make number cards from 0 to 9. The
game rule is that each number can be used
only once.

1. Write the greatest possible 5-digit number. _____

2. Write the least possible 5-digit number. _____

3. Use six cards to show the greatest
   possible sum.

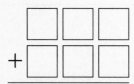

4. Use six cards to show the least
   possible sum.

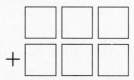

5. Fill in the missing numbers.

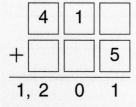

6. Fill in the missing numbers.

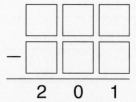

Practice

Here are three practice problems for you.

Quick-Solve 1

Use cards from 0–9. Suppose you turn over an 8. Where would you put it on the grid to get the **least** possible sum? Why?

```
  4 □ 5
+ □ 7 □
```

Quick-Solve 2

Use cards from 0–9. Suppose you are trying to find the **least** possible difference. What card would you use? Why?

```
  8 7
- □ 3
```

Quick-Solve 3

Will this arrangement of 7, 6, 3, and 4 give you the **greatest** possible sum? How do you know?

```
  7 6
+ 3 4
```

Use What You Know

Use logical reasoning to solve these number riddles.

> **B**rad is going to have a party. The date on the invitation is a riddle. When is Brad's party?

It's a Party!

Where: Brad's House

Date: The day of the month is an odd number. It has a 2 and a number greater than 7. Most years, this day does not exist.

1. On what day is Brad's party? _____

2. In which month is Brad's party? How do you know?

   _____

   _____

3. Allison asks Brad for his house number. Brad answers, "The house number is two odd numbers together. The lower number is first. Their sum is 36. Their product is 323."

   What is Brad's house number? _____

4. At the party, Allison starts a game of *What's My Number?* She says, "My house number is the same forward as backward. There are three digits. The number is the product of an odd number multiplied by itself."

   What is Allison's house number? _____

Lesson 4   Solve It Your Way

Read each problem and decide how you will find the solution.

You may want to choose one of these strategies for each problem.

Find a Pattern
Use Logical Reasoning

1. Whitney notices that the street addresses follow a pattern. She passes 34 Front Street, 26 Front Street, and 18 Front Street. What will the next street address be?

2. Use numbers 0 to 5. Do not use any number more than once. What is the greatest possible number?

3. Brittany plays the *What's My Number?* game with George. The pattern is "Multiply by 4." How will Brittany answer when George says 8?

4. In a *What's My Number?* game, Jordan says 45 and Tony answers 5. When Jordan says 27, Tony says 3. What could the pattern be?

5. Suppose you play *The Greatest Possible Sum* game. You use cards from 0–9. What numbers can you use to make the greatest possible sum?

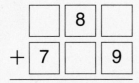

6. Daniel's age is an odd number less than ten. His age can be divided by 3, but he is not 3. How old is Daniel?

Practice

Now write your own problems.

Quick-Solve 1
The answer to a problem is, "The pattern is add 5." What might the question be? Write your own problem to share with a friend. If your friend does not find the pattern, discuss how you might change the problem or the solution to match.

Quick-Solve 2
The missing number in the middle of the pattern is 15. What might the pattern be? Share the pattern with a friend. If he or she cannot find the missing number, discuss how you might change the problem.

Quick-Solve 3
The answer to a problem is 543. What might the question be? Write your own addition problem with missing numbers. Share it with a friend. If he or she cannot find the missing numbers, discuss how you might change the problem.

Applying Strategies

Review   Show What You Know

Play the *What's My Number?* game with a partner. Choose a pattern. Write three numbers in your pattern. Ask your partner to guess what comes next.

1. My pattern is: _____ , _____ , _____

2. What comes next? _____

Now let your partner write a pattern. It's your turn to guess what comes next.

3. The pattern is: _____ , _____ , _____

4. What comes next? _____

5. Now work together to write a pattern that makes you add, subtract, add, subtract, and keep going. Share your pattern with someone else.

_____ , _____ , _____ , _____ , _____ ,

Read each problem. Then solve.

Wow! You can choose from all these strategies!

Make a Model
Make an Estimate
Find a Pattern
Use Logical Reasoning

1. A Pony Express rider traveled 130 miles from Fort Bridger to South Pass. He rode 279 miles from South Pass to Fort Laramie. How far did he ride from Fort Bridger to Fort Laramie?

2. The first wagon in the wagon train was carrying 683 pounds of supplies. The next wagon had 592 pounds of supplies. About how many pounds of supplies did they carry in all?

3. James plays a game called *Get to 1,000.* He uses the number cards 0, 1, 2, 3, 4, 5, 6, 7, 8, and 9. How close can he get to 1,000?

4. Karen plays *Get to 1,000* with number cards from 0 to 9. She draws 3, 4, and 8. What 3 cards will give her a sum of 1,000?

5. Josh plays *Get to 100*. He uses cards from 0 to 9. Choose 4 cards he could draw that will give him a sum of exactly 100. Show your addition problem below.

6. Helen uses cards from 0 to 9. What number cards does she need to draw to find the greatest possible difference?

7. Darius gives every twelfth person in line a free juice. Suppose he gives the 1st, 13th, and 25th person a free drink. What is the number of the next person in line who will get a free drink?

8. What are the next three numbers in the pattern?

30, 33, 31, 34

_____, _____, _____

What is the pattern?

_____

9. What are the next two numbers in the pattern?

2, 1, 4, 3, 6, 5, _____, _____

What is the pattern?

_____

10. What are the next two numbers in the pattern?

320, 160, 80, 40, _____, _____

What is the pattern?

_____

UNIT 3 Let's Play Ball!

Lesson 1   Write a Plan

Suppose there are 153 baseball players in a league. If there are 9 players on each team, how many teams can you make?

Write a plan to solve the problem.

Step 1   Write in your own words what you need to find out.

_____

_____

Step 2   Write the facts that will be useful.

_____

_____

Step 3   Explain or show how you will solve the problem.

_____

_____

_____

_____

_____

_____

Choose the Operation

Try choosing an operation to solve the problem.

Multiply to combine equal groups. Divide to separate into equal groups.

Choose whether to multiply or divide to find the number of teams you can make with 153 players. Multiply and divide the numbers in the problem. Look at both solutions. Read the problem again. Check which solution is reasonable. If there are 9 players on a team, how many teams can you make?

1. If you multiply, what answer do you get?

$$\begin{array}{r} 153 \\ \times\ 9 \\ \hline \end{array}$$

2. If you divide, what answer do you get?

$$9\overline{)153}$$

3. Read the problem again. Which solution is reasonable? How do you know?

_____

_____

_____

4. How many teams can you make? _____ teams

5. There are 8 softball teams. How many softball players are there, if there are 10 players on a team?

_____

_____

_____

Practice

Here are three practice problems for you.

Quick-Solve 1

Suppose it costs $8 to watch a baseball game. How much will a family of 6 pay?

Quick-Solve 2

The store manager said to Chanda, "Please arrange these baseball shirts equally on 3 racks." Chanda counted 102 shirts. Could Chanda arrange the shirts equally on the racks? How do you know?

Quick-Solve 3

A store window has a display of boxes of sneakers. There are 45 rows of boxes. There are 5 boxes in each row. How many boxes are there in the display?

Applying Strategies

Use What You Know

Joanne plays softball 3 times a week. How many times does she play in 12 weeks?

If you need help, look back to pages 34 and 35.

Choose whether to multiply or divide to find the number of times Joanne plays softball in 12 weeks. Multiply and divide the numbers in the problem. Look at both solutions. Read the problem again. Check which solution is reasonable. If Joanne plays 3 times a week, how many times does she play in 12 weeks?

1. If you multiply, what answer do you get?

$$\begin{array}{r} 12 \\ \times 3 \\ \hline \end{array}$$

2. If you divide, what answer do you get?

$$3\overline{)12}$$

3. Read the problem again. Which solution is reasonable? How do you know?

_____

_____

4. In 12 weeks, how many times does Joanne play softball?

_____ times

5. The distance between each base on a softball field is 60 feet. How far would you run from first base to third base?

_____

_____

Lesson 2 Write a Plan

You have 92 baseballs and many boxes.
You want to pack 8 baseballs into each box.
How many boxes can you pack?

WILL there be any baseballs left over?

Write a plan to solve the problem.

Step 1 Write in your own words what you need to find out.

_____

_____

_____

Step 2 Write the facts that will be useful.

_____

_____

_____

Step 3 Explain or show how you will solve the problem.

_____

_____

_____

_____

_____

_____

_____

_____

Choose the Operation

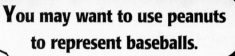

You may want to use peanuts to represent baseballs.

Try choosing an operation to solve the problem.

Choose whether to multiply or divide to find the number of boxes with 8 baseballs. Multiply and divide the numbers in the problem. Look at both solutions. Read the problem again. Check which solution is reasonable.

How many boxes can you pack with 8 baseballs?

1. If you multiply, what answer do you get?

$$\begin{array}{r} 92 \\ \times 8 \\ \hline \end{array}$$

2. If you divide, what answer do you get?

$$8\overline{)92}$$

3. Read the problem again. Which solution is reasonable? How do you know?

_____

_____

4. How many boxes can you pack with 8 baseballs? How do you know?

_____

_____

5. Ms. Owen has 45 students in her sports club. Ms. Owen plans to put 6 students on each team. She wants all the students to be on a team. Will her plan work? Why or why not?

_____

_____

Practice

Here are three practice problems for you.

Quick-Solve 1

A store has 4 shelves. The store manager wants you to put 18 pairs of sneakers on each shelf. Will you put more or less than 100 pairs of shoes on the shelves? How do you know?

Quick-Solve 2

A baseball has 216 stitches. Adam said, "There are 844 stitches on 4 baseballs." Adam is not right. Explain his error.

Quick-Solve 3

You have 32 piles of sweaters with 2 in each pile. Could you rearrange the sweaters in 16 piles with 4 in each pile? Why or why not?

Use What You Know

Frank brought cookies to his team's party.
If there are 18 cookies in each bag, how many
cookies are in 6 bags?

If you need help, look back to pages 38 and 39.

Choose whether to multiply or divide to find the number of
cookies in 6 bags. Multiply and divide the numbers in the
problem. Look at both solutions. Read the problem again.
Check which solution is reasonable.
How many cookies are in 6 bags?

1. If you multiply, what answer do
you get?

$$\begin{array}{r} 18 \\ \times 6 \\ \hline \end{array}$$

2. If you divide, what answer do
you get?

$$6\overline{)18}$$

3. Read the problem again. Which solution is reasonable?
How do you know?

_____

_____

4. How many cookies are in 6 bags? _____ cookies

5. The coach had 4 bags with 6 large-size shirts in each
bag. He had 6 bags with 4 small-size shirts in each
bag. Did he have the same number of large-size and
small-size shirts? How do you know?

_____

_____

_____

_____

Lesson 3   Solve Multi-Step Problems

You learned how to choose the operation to solve problems. Now try solving this multi-step problem.

Sometimes you need to solve more than one problem to answer a question.

Jon has two baseball albums. The National League album has 8 sheets with 9 cards in each sheet. The American League album has 12 sheets with 9 cards in each sheet. How many cards does he have in all?

1. How many cards are in the National League album? _____ cards
   Show your work here.

2. How many cards are in the American League album? _____ cards
   Show your work here.

3. How many cards does Jon have in all? _____ cards
   Show your work here.

4. Suppose Jon trades 6 of his National League cards for 12 American League cards. How many cards will he have in each album? How do you know?

   _____

   _____

Solving Multi-Step Problems: Multiplication and Division

Practice

Here are three practice problems for you.

Quick-Solve 1

A store has 2 racks with 12 orange jackets each. It also has 4 racks with 15 blue jackets each. How many jackets are there in all?

Quick-Solve 2

Kim works at a sports store. She works 3 hours on Wednesday and 5 hours on Saturday. She gets paid $9 an hour. How much does she earn in one week?

Quick-Solve 3

Which is a better buy? How do you know?

5 baseballs for $10⁰⁰

6 baseballs for $10⁸⁰

Use What You Know

Now try solving another multi-step problem.

How much will batting practice cost for a family with 2 adults and 3 children?

Batting Practice
$8 per Child
$12 per Adult
$6 per Senior Citizen

1. How much will it cost for the children to bat? $_____
Show your work here.

2. How much will it cost for the adults to bat? $_____
Show your work here.

3. How much will it cost the family to bat? $_____
Show your work here.

4. Suppose you plan a fun day with friends. If there are 3
senior citizens, 2 adults, and 6 children, how much will
it cost for batting practice? How do you know?

_____

_____

_____

Lesson 4 Solve It Your Way

Read each problem and decide how you will find the solution.

You may want to choose one of these strategies for each problem.

Choose the Operation
Solve Multi-Step Problems

1. If there are 6 teams with 9 players on each team, how many players are there?

2. Coach Jackson bought 4 baseballs for $5 each and 2 baseballs for $8 each. How much did she spend?

3. A baseball weighs about 5 oz. If you have about a pound of baseballs, about how many baseballs do you have? [Hint: 1 lb = 16 oz]

4. In 1993, Mark Whitten scored 4 home runs for St. Louis in one game. If the distance between each base is 90 feet, how far did he run?

5. In a Little League baseball field, the distance between bases is 60 feet. In a Major League baseball field, the distance between bases is 90 feet. How much longer is a Major League home run than a Little League home run?

6. You have 96 baseball caps. You sell 3 bags with 6 caps in each bag, and 2 bags with 8 caps in each bag. How many caps do you have left?

Practice

Now write your own problems using multiplication or division.

Quick-Solve 1

The answer to a problem is 12 baseballs. Write your own problem to share with a friend. If your friend does not get an answer of 12, discuss how you might change the problem or the solution to match.

Quick-Solve 2

The answer to a problem is 7 gloves. Write your own problem to share with a friend. If your friend does not get an answer of 7, discuss how you might change the problem or the solution to match.

Quick-Solve 3

The answer to a problem is 96 players. Write your own problem to share with a friend. If your friend does not get an answer of 96, discuss how you might change the problem or the solution to match.

Review   Show What You Know

Work in a small group. Suppose a store manager asks you to arrange 36 baseball shirts. She wants you to make equal stacks.

1. Complete the table. Find the different ways you can put 36 shirts into equal stacks.

Number of Stacks	Number in Each Stack

2. How many different ways can you stack 36 shirts? _____ ways

3. If each shirt costs $12, how much will all the shirts cost?

_____

_____

4. Suppose the store paid $252 for all 36 shirts. What operation should you choose to find the cost of 1 shirt? How much did the store pay for each shirt?

_____

_____

UNIT 4 Fun and Games

Lesson 1 Write a Plan

You have 2 counters. They are both yellow on one side and green on the other. Toss both counters. Are they more likely to land with the yellow sides up, green sides up, or one of each? How can you find out?

Write a plan to solve the problem.

Step 1 Write in your own words what you need to find out.

_____

_____

Step 2 Write the facts that will be useful.

_____

_____

Step 3 Explain or show how you will solve the problem.

_____
_____
_____
_____
_____
_____
_____

Writing a Plan: Data and Probability

Make a Table

Try making a table to solve the problem.

A probability can be stated as a fraction and reduced.
2 out of 8 $= \frac{2}{8} = \frac{1}{4}$

Predict which combinations you are more likely to toss. Then test your prediction. Make a tally table. Toss the counters 20 times. Record each toss in your table.

1. Toss the counters 20 times. Complete the table. Record the outcome of each toss with a tally mark.

Color	My Guess	Tally Marks	Outcomes	Fractions
Both Green	_____ out of 20		_____ out of 20	
Both Yellow	_____ out of 20		_____ out of 20	
One Green, One Yellow	_____ out of 20		_____ out of 20	

2. Write the number of tally marks for each outcome. Then write each outcome as a fraction in simplest terms.

3. Are all the outcomes the same? Explain why you think this happened.

_____

_____

4. Compare your outcomes and a friend's outcomes.

Are they the same or different? _____

5. Do you think that the outcomes are more accurate if you make 20 tosses or 100 tosses? Why?

_____

_____

Practice

Here are three practice problems for you.

Quick-Solve 1

You have 2 counters. They are both yellow on one side and red on the other. If you toss both counters thirty times, what is the probability of tossing two red sides up?

Color	Tally Marks	Outcomes	Fractions
Both red			
Both yellow			
One red, One yellow			

Quick-Solve 2

You have 2 counters. One is yellow on both sides. One is yellow and blue. Toss both counters 10 times. What is the probability of both landing with yellow sides up?

Color	Tally Marks	Outcomes	Fractions
Both yellow			
One yellow, One blue			

Quick-Solve 3

Use the same counters as in Quick-Solve 2. This time, toss them 40 times. Are the outcomes the same? Why do you think this happened?

Color	Tally Marks	Outcomes	Fractions
Both yellow			
One yellow, One blue			

Use What You Know

Try a different kind of game to predict outcomes.

Remember when you predict you are guessing what will happen.

Make a tally table. Write each letter of the word A-P-P-L-E on a separate card. Without looking, pick a card. Record the letter you picked in a tally table. Which letter are you more likely to pick?

1. Test your prediction. Pick a card 20 times. After each time, put all the cards together again and shuffle them. Make a tally mark for each letter.

Letter	My Guess	Tally Marks	Outcomes	Fractions
A	_____ out of 20		_____ out of 20	
P	_____ out of 20		_____ out of 20	
L	_____ out of 20		_____ out of 20	
E	_____ out of 20		_____ out of 20	

2. Count the tally marks and complete the table. Write each outcome as a fraction in simplest terms.

3. Which letter has the most tally marks? How does this compare with your prediction? _____

_____

4. What is the probability of picking a card marked P? _____ out of 5 = _____

Explain your answer. _____

_____

Lesson 2 Write a Plan

Sunny, Derek, and Tracy want to play a game with two counters. Both counters are yellow on one side and green on the other. To get a point, Sunny needs 2 yellow counters. Derek needs 1 yellow and 1 green counter. Tracy needs 2 green counters. Is this a fair or unfair game?

Write a plan to solve the problem.

Step 1   Write in your own words what you need to find out.

_____

_____

Step 2   Write the facts that will be useful.

_____

_____

Step 3   Explain or show how you will solve the problem.

_____

_____

_____

_____

_____

_____

_____

Make a Table

Try making a table to solve the problem.

> In a fair game, each player has an equal chance to win.

Toss the counters to see who gets a point. The first person to get 5 points wins. Is the game fair or unfair?

1. Play the game for Sunny, Derek, and Tracy.
Record each toss with a tally mark.

Player	What is Needed	Tally Points
Sunny	2 yellow counters	
Derek	1 yellow counter, 1 green counter	
Tracy	2 green counters	

2. Which player was first to get 5 points? _____

3. Count the total number of times you tossed the counters. _____

4. Now write fractions for each outcome.
The total number of tosses is the denominator.

Sunny _____   Derek _____   Tracy _____

5. Is this game fair or unfair? How do you know?

_____

6. What if Derek did not play? Would the game be fair then?
How do you know?

_____

_____

Practice

Here are three practice problems for you.

Quick-Solve 1

Jenny and Katie are playing a game with 4 red counters and 6 blue counters in a bag. Jenny gets a point when red is drawn. Katie gets a point for blue. All the counters are put in the bag after each turn. Is the game fair or unfair? Try 20 times. Show your work in the table.

Player	What is Needed	Tally Points
Jenny	red	
Katie	blue	

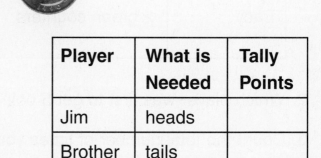

Quick-Solve 2

Jim and his brother are tossing a coin to see who will do the dishes. Jim says, "Heads I win, tails you win." Should his brother agree? Try this 10 times. Show your work in the table.

Player	What is Needed	Tally Points
Jim	heads	
Brother	tails	

Quick-Solve 3

Tom and Anna are playing a game with a number cube labeled 1 to 6. They roll the number cube. Tom gets 1 point if the number is odd. Anna gets 1 point if the number is even. Is the game fair or unfair? Try it. Show your work in the table.

Player	What is Needed	Tally Points
Tom	odd	
Anna	even	

Use What You Know

> **The first person to get 5 points wins.**

Play another game with different counters. One is yellow on both sides. The other is yellow and green. To get a point, Sunny needs yellow, yellow. Derek needs yellow, green. Tracy needs green, green. Is the game fair or unfair?

1. Play the game. Record each toss with a tally mark.

Player	What is Needed	Tally Points
Sunny	2 yellow counters	
Derek	1 yellow counter, 1 green counter	
Tracy	2 green counters	

2. Which person was the first to get 5 points? _____

3. Count the total number of times you tossed the counters. _____

4. Now write fractions for each outcome.
The total number of tosses is the denominator.

Sunny _____   Derek _____   Tracy _____

5. Is this game fair or unfair? How do you know?

_____

6. Tracy said, "I can never get a point!" Is she correct?
How do you know?

_____

_____

Lesson 3 Make an Organized List

You have used a table to solve probability problems. Now try making an organized list to solve a problem.

Play a game with 2 counters. One counter is blue on one side and yellow on the other. The other counter is red on one side and yellow on the other. If you toss both counters, how many possible outcomes are there?

1. Start with the blue and yellow counter. If the blue side comes up, list the possible outcomes of the red and yellow counter.

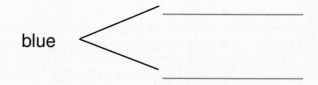

blue

2. If the yellow side of the first counter comes up, list the possible outcomes of the red and yellow counter.

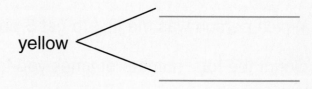

yellow

3. How many possible outcomes are there? _____

4. What are the chances of tossing two yellow counters? _____ out of _____ How do you know?

_____

_____

_____

Practice

Here are three practice problems for you.

Quick-Solve 1
Look at the spinners. List all the possible outcomes of spinning both of them together. How many possible outcomes are there?

Spinner A   **Spinner B**

Quick-Solve 2
A store sells sunglasses. They come in three colors: red, blue, and green. They come in round or square frames. How many possible choices are there? Make a list to show the choices.

Quick-Solve 3
Suppose you rolled two number cubes labeled from 1 to 6. Then you added the numbers you rolled. How many ways could you roll a sum of 6? Make a list.

Use What You Know

Now make another organized list to find possible outcomes.

How many possible outcomes are there if you spin both spinners together?

Spinner A   **Spinner B**

1. Start with the red and blue spinner. If it lands on red first, list the possible outcomes of the other spinner.

red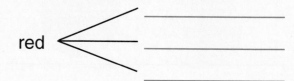

2. If the spinner lands on the blue part of the first spinner, list the possible outcomes of the other spinner.

blue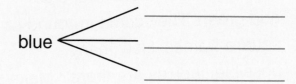

3. How many possible outcomes are there? _____

4. What are the chances of both spinners pointing to the same color? _____ out of _____ How do you know?

_____

_____

_____

Lesson 4   Solve It Your Way

Read each problem and decide how you will find the solution.

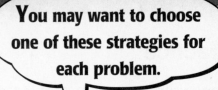

You may want to choose one of these strategies for each problem.

Make a Table
Make an Organized List

---

1. Sean is reaching into a bag of 6 bagels. There are 5 plain bagels and 1 onion bagel. What is the probability that Sean will pick an onion bagel?

_____ out of 6 = _____

2. There are 11 girls in a class of 29 students. The teacher puts each student's name in a hat. Suppose she pulls a student's name out of a hat without looking. Is it more or less likely it will be a girl's name?

---

3. If you toss one coin, what is the probability of tossing a head?

4. If you toss two coins, what are all the possible outcomes?

---

5. Tomoko and Lynn play a game with a number cube labeled from 1 to 6. Tomoko gets one point if the number is less than 4. Lynn gets one point if the number is greater than 3. Is the game fair? Explain.

6. Mia gets 1 point if the spinner lands on red. Bob gets 1 point if it lands on blue. Is the game fair? Explain.

Practice

Now write your own problems using probability.

Quick-Solve 1

The answer is "1 out of 4." What might the question be? Write your own problem to share with a friend. If your friend does not get an answer of "1 out of 4," discuss how you might change the problem or the solution to match.

Quick-Solve 2

The answer is "3 out of 30." What might the question be? Write your own problem to share with a friend. If your friend does not get an answer of "3 out of 30," discuss how you might change the problem or the solution to match.

Quick-Solve 3

The answer is "1 out of 2." What might the question be? Write your own problem to share with a friend. If your friend does not get an answer of "1 out of 2," discuss how you might change the problem or the solution to match.

Review   Show What You Know

Work in a small group. Give each group member five blank cards. Have each person write *red* or *blue* on each card. They may write the same color on each card or mix them up.

1. Put all the cards in a paper bag. Without looking, draw out 4 cards. Use tally marks to show the outcome. Do not put the cards back in the bag.

Color	Tally Marks
Red	
Blue	

2. Make a prediction. Do you think there are more cards that have the word *red* or *blue*?

_____

_____

3. Draw out 10 more cards. Add to the tally marks on your chart to count these. Did the outcome match your prediction? Explain why or why not.

_____

_____

_____

4. Put all the cards back in the bag. List the possible outcomes of just drawing two cards.

_____ and _____

_____ and _____

_____ and _____

Review   Units 3–4

Read each problem and decide how you will find the solution.

You may want to choose one of these strategies for each problem.

Choose the Operation
Solve Multi-Step Problems
Make a Table
Make an Organized List

1. A bike race raises money. A sponsor will pay $2.00 for each mile that riders travel. This year, there are 95 riders in the race. They each travel 5 miles. How much money do they raise?

2. Martha is saving money for a new bike. The bike costs $250.00. She saves $5.00 each week. How many weeks will it take her to save the money?

3. At the School Safety Day event, there were 32 tricycles and 44 bicycles. How many wheels were at Safety Day?

4. In Los Angeles, California, it rains about 3 days out of every month. Write this as a fraction in lowest terms. Use the number of days in April as an example.

5. Suppose you toss 2 number cubes labeled 1 to 6. Then you add the numbers. What is the greatest sum you can get?

6. Ivan earns $7.00 an hour. He worked 10 hours one week. He worked 12 hours the next week. How much did he earn in all?

Cumulative Review: Applying Strategies

7. Kyoko has a red shirt, a blue shirt, black pants and blue pants. Make a list to show how many outfits she can make from these items.

8. A cafe sells blueberry muffins and banana nut muffins. They also have milk, apple juice, and orange juice. Make a list to show how many choices you can have for one muffin and something to drink.

9. Kim places two blue counters and six red ones in a paper bag. What is the chance that the first counter she pulls out will be red? Make a table or a list to show your work. Write this as a fraction in simplest terms.

10. Eric is working in his aunt's store. The first day he makes only $1.00. Every day, his pay doubles. How much will he make on day 10? Make a table or a list to show your work.

UNIT 5 — A Fence for Fido

Lesson 1 Write a Plan

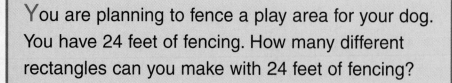

You are planning to fence a play area for your dog. You have 24 feet of fencing. How many different rectangles can you make with 24 feet of fencing?

Write a plan to solve the problem.

Step 1 Write in your own words what you need to find out.

_____

_____

_____

Step 2 Write the facts that will be useful.

_____

_____

_____

Step 3 Explain or show how you will solve the problem.

_____

_____

_____

_____

_____

_____

Draw a Picture

Remember that opposite sides of a rectangle have the same length.

Try drawing a picture to solve the problem.

> **D**raw each possible rectangle for 24 feet of fencing. Let the distance between each dot represent one foot. How many different rectangles can you make?

1. Draw each rectangle on the dot paper below.

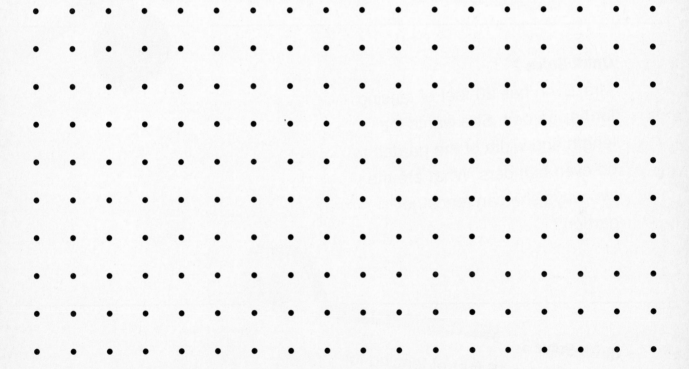

2. How do you know that each rectangle is 24 units around?

_____

_____

_____

3. How many rectangles can you make with 24 feet of fencing?

_____ rectangles

Practice

Here are three practice problems for you.

Quick-Solve 1

Mr. Lopez has a rectangular flower garden. The garden is long and narrow. It has 26 feet of bricks around the edge. What is a possible length and width of the garden?

Quick-Solve 2

Mrs. Even has 20 feet of fencing for her garden. She wants the length and width of the garden to be even numbers. What are the two ways she can fence her garden?

Quick-Solve 3

Mrs. Odd has 16 feet of fencing for her garden. She wants a square garden, but only if the sides are odd numbers. Can she use all of the fencing and do this?

Applying Strategies

Use What You Know

What if you had 20 feet of fencing?

Draw each possible rectangle for 20 feet of
fencing. Let the distance between the dots
represent feet. How many different rectangles
can you make?

If you need help, look back
to pages 64 and 65.

1. Draw each rectangle on the dot paper below.

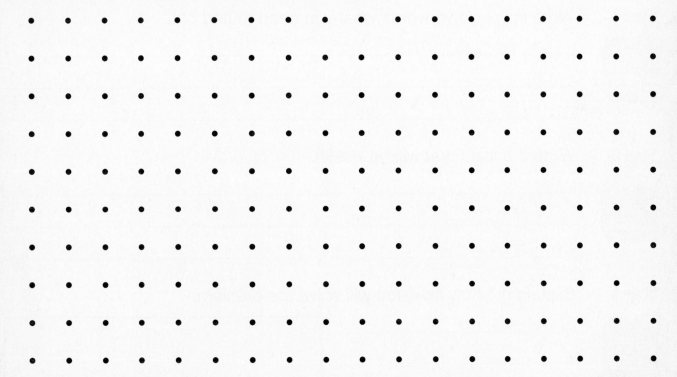

2. How many rectangles can you make with 20 feet of fencing?

_____ rectangles

3. Could you make a rectangle with 21 feet of fencing?
Why or why not?

_____

_____

_____

Lesson 2   Write a Plan

Suppose you could buy a ready-made dog yard. One model is 5 feet wide and 7 feet long. The other model is 6 feet on every side. Which yard would give the dog the biggest play area? How do you know?

Area is the amount of room inside a figure.

Write a plan to solve the problem.

Step 1   Write in your own words what you need to find out.

_____

_____

_____

Step 2   Write the facts that will be useful.

_____

_____

_____

Step 3   Explain or show how you will solve the problem.

Draw a Picture

Try drawing a picture to solve the area problem.

Try using dot paper to draw each fenced yard. Make sure that one rectangle has sides of 5 units and 7 units. The other yard has 6 units on each side. Draw lines between all the dots. Then count the squares inside each yard. The yard with the most squares inside has the greater area.

You may want to check your answer by placing centimeter cubes inside each yard area.

1. Draw each rectangle on the dot paper below.

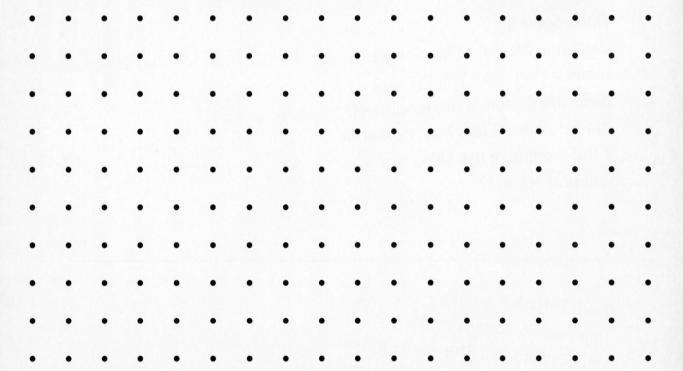

2. Which rectangle has the greater area, 5 × 7 or 6 × 6? How do you know?

_____

_____

_____

Practice

Here are three practice problems for you.

Quick-Solve 1

Ann's flower garden has an area of 20 square feet. What is the length and width of her garden? Can you figure out all three possible solutions?

Quick-Solve 2

Jake has 28 feet of fencing to make a dog yard. Will the dog have more room if the lengths of the sides are 2 feet and 12 feet or if the lengths of the sides are 4 feet and 10 feet?

Quick-Solve 3

Tara has 25 square cement stepping stones. She wants to use every stone to make a patio. How can she arrange the stones to make the patio square? Write the length and the width.

Use What You Know

If you need help, look back to pages 68 and 69.

Martin and Carrie must weed their gardens. Martin's garden is 3 feet wide and 10 feet long. Carrie's garden is 2 feet wide and 14 feet long. Who has more garden to weed?

1. Draw each rectangle on the dot paper below.

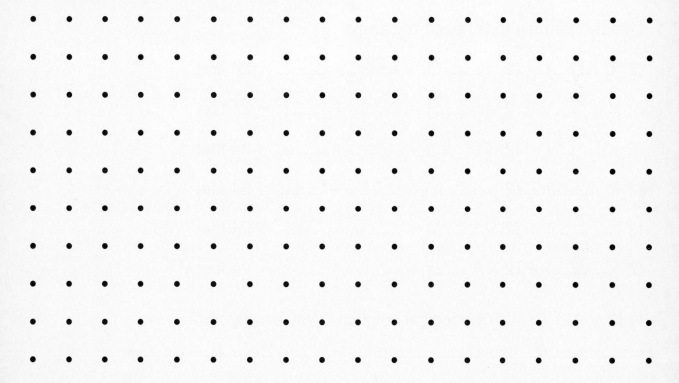

2. Which rectangle has the greater area, 3 × 10 or 2 × 14? How do you know?

_____

_____

_____

Lesson 3   Use a Formula

You have drawn pictures on dot paper to solve problems.
Now try using a formula to solve a problem.

> You have 24 feet of fencing to make a dog yard.
> How many different rectangles could you make?

For a rectangle, you can use this formula.
(2 × length) + (2 × width) = perimeter

1. Use the formula to list each rectangle.

(2 × __11__) + (2 × __1__) = __22__ + __2__ = 24 feet

(2 × _____) + (2 × _____) = _____ + _____ = 24 feet

(2 × _____) + (2 × _____) = _____ + _____ = 24 feet

(2 × _____) + (2 × _____) = _____ + _____ = 24 feet

(2 × _____) + (2 × _____) = _____ + _____ = 24 feet

(2 × _____) + (2 × _____) = _____ + _____ = 24 feet

2. Is (2 × 12) + (2 × 0) a logical solution? Why or why not?

_____

_____

_____

3. How many rectangles can you make with 20 feet of fencing?
Make a list. Circle the solution that would make a square.

(2 × _____) + (2 × _____) = 20   (2 × _____) + (2 × _____) = 20

(2 × _____) + (2 × _____) = 20   (2 × _____) + (2 × _____) = 20

(2 × _____) + (2 × _____) = 20   (2 × _____) + (2 × _____) = 20

Using a Formula: Perimeter

Practice

Here are three practice problems for you.

Quick-Solve 1

Mr. Adams wants to fence a square section of his yard for a dog pen. He has 34 feet of fencing. What is the largest square he can make and have the least leftover fencing?

Quick-Solve 2

Mr. McNeil wants to make a rectangular dog yard with 31 feet of fencing. Can he use all the fencing with none left over? What if he adds a gate that is 3 feet wide?

Quick-Solve 3

Mrs. Lewis wants to put a wallpaper border around her living room. The room is 15 feet long and 13 feet wide. How many feet of bordering does she need?

Use What You Know

You learned how to use a formula to find perimeter. Now try using a formula to find area.

The space inside a rectangle is called its *area*.

> You want to make a dog yard that has an area of 48 square feet. How many different rectangles could you make?

Use this formula to find the area of a rectangle.

length × width = area

1. Use the formula to list each rectangle.

_____ × _____ = 48 square feet   _____ × _____ = 48 square feet

_____ × _____ = 48 square feet   _____ × _____ = 48 square feet

_____ × _____ = 48 square feet

2. Which of the above dog yards would use the most fencing? _____

How did you find out? _____

_____

3. Tyler's dog yard is 9 feet long and 12 feet wide.

What is the area? _____

4. Emily's dog yard is a square. One side is 16 feet long.

What is the area? _____

5. Lashawna's garden is 15 feet long and 2 feet wide.

What is the area? _____

6. The length of Jose's garden is 10 feet. The area is 30 square feet.

What is the width of Jose's garden?

_____